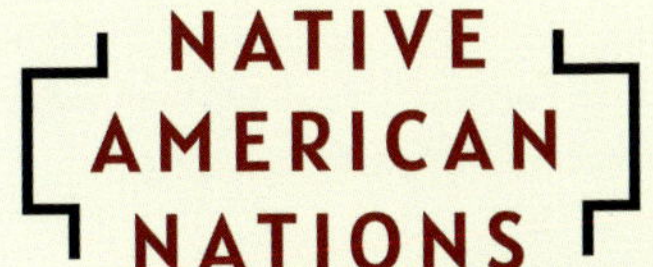

Blackfoot

F.A. BIRD

Checkerboard Library

An Imprint of Abdo Publishing
abdobooks.com

ABDOBOOKS.COM
Published by Abdo Publishing, a division of ABDO, PO Box 398166, Minneapolis, Minnesota 55439.

Printed in the United States of America, North Mankato, Minnesota
102024
012025

Editors: Lauri Nelson
Design: Mighty Media, Inc.

Cover Photograph: Eye Ubiquitous/Universal Images Group via Getty Images
Interior Photographs: Ad_hominem/Shutterstock Images, p. 7; Artur Widak/NurPhoto via Getty Images, p. 5; Danita Delimont Photography/Newscom, p. 19; Gendreau Collection/Getty Images, p. 23; George Ostertag/Alamy Stock Photo, p. 25; Ronnie Chua/Shutterstock Images, p. 17; T. Ulrich/Classicstock/Getty Images, p. 21; The Picture Art Collection/Alamy Stock Photo, p. 27; Tommy Martino/University of Montana/Getty Images, p. 29; Visual Studies Workshop/Getty Images, p. 11; Walter McClintock Papers. Yale Collection of Western Americana, Beinecke Rare Book and Manuscript Library, pp. 9, 13; Werner Forman/Universal Images Group/Getty Images, p. 15

Library of Congress Control Number: 2024938795

Publisher's Cataloging-in-Publication Data
Names: Bird, F.A., author.
Title: Blackfoot / by F.A. Bird
Description: Minneapolis, Minnesota : ABDO Publishing, 2025 | Series: Native American nations | Includes online resources and index.
Identifiers: ISBN 9781098296193 (lib. bdg.) | ISBN 9798384917304 (ebook)
Subjects: LCSH: Blackfoot Indians (Algonquian)--Juvenile literature. | Siksika Indians--Juvenile literature. | Sihasapa Indians--Juvenile literature. | Native Americans--Juvenile literature. | Indians of North America--Juvenile literature. | Indigenous peoples--Social life and customs--Juvenile literature. | Cultural anthropology--Juvenile literature.
Classification: DDC 973.0497--dc23

Contents

Homelands ... 4
Society ... 6
Homes ... 8
Food ... 10
Clothing ... 12
Crafts ... 14
Family ... 16
Children ... 18
Traditions ... 20
War ... 22
Contact with Europeans ... 24
Crowfoot ... 26
The Blackfoot Today ... 28
Glossary ... 30
Online Resources ... 31
Index ... 32

Homelands

The Blackfoot call themselves *Niitsitapi* (neet-see-TAH-pee), which means "the Real People." They are a **confederacy** of four tribes. The tribes are called the Siksika (SIK-seek-ah), the Blood or Kainai (GAY-nah), the Piikani (Pee-GAN-nee), and the Pikuni. The Blackfoot language is called Blackfoot. It is from the Algonquian family.

The Blackfoot lived in present-day northern Montana and southern Canada. Their land covered a large area. Blackfoot territory may have reached from present-day North Dakota west to the Rocky Mountains. To the north, their land reached Alberta and Saskatchewan in Canada. The Blackfoot homelands had high, rolling plains. They also had forests, grasslands, streams, and rivers. Hills, rugged glaciers, and steep cliffs also covered the land.

The Writing-on-Stone Provincial Park in Alberta, Canada, holds many protected First Nations' petroglyphs (rock carvings) and pictographs (rock paintings).

Society

The Blackfoot lived together in bands. The members worked together to feed and defend the people. If people were unhappy with their group, they were free to leave and join another band.

Each band's people chose a chief. He had to be a good warrior, and be generous to his people. Each band also had a war chief, a peace chief, and a council of elders.

Blackfoot bands had many societies. The members of each society had special duties. The military societies protected the people and enforced the traditional laws. The religious societies and women's societies performed ceremonies.

Occasionally Blackfoot bands gathered together. They joined forces to protect their land and people from harm. The chiefs often met to discuss important matters. The Blackfoot also gathered for special ceremonies, such as the Sun Dance.

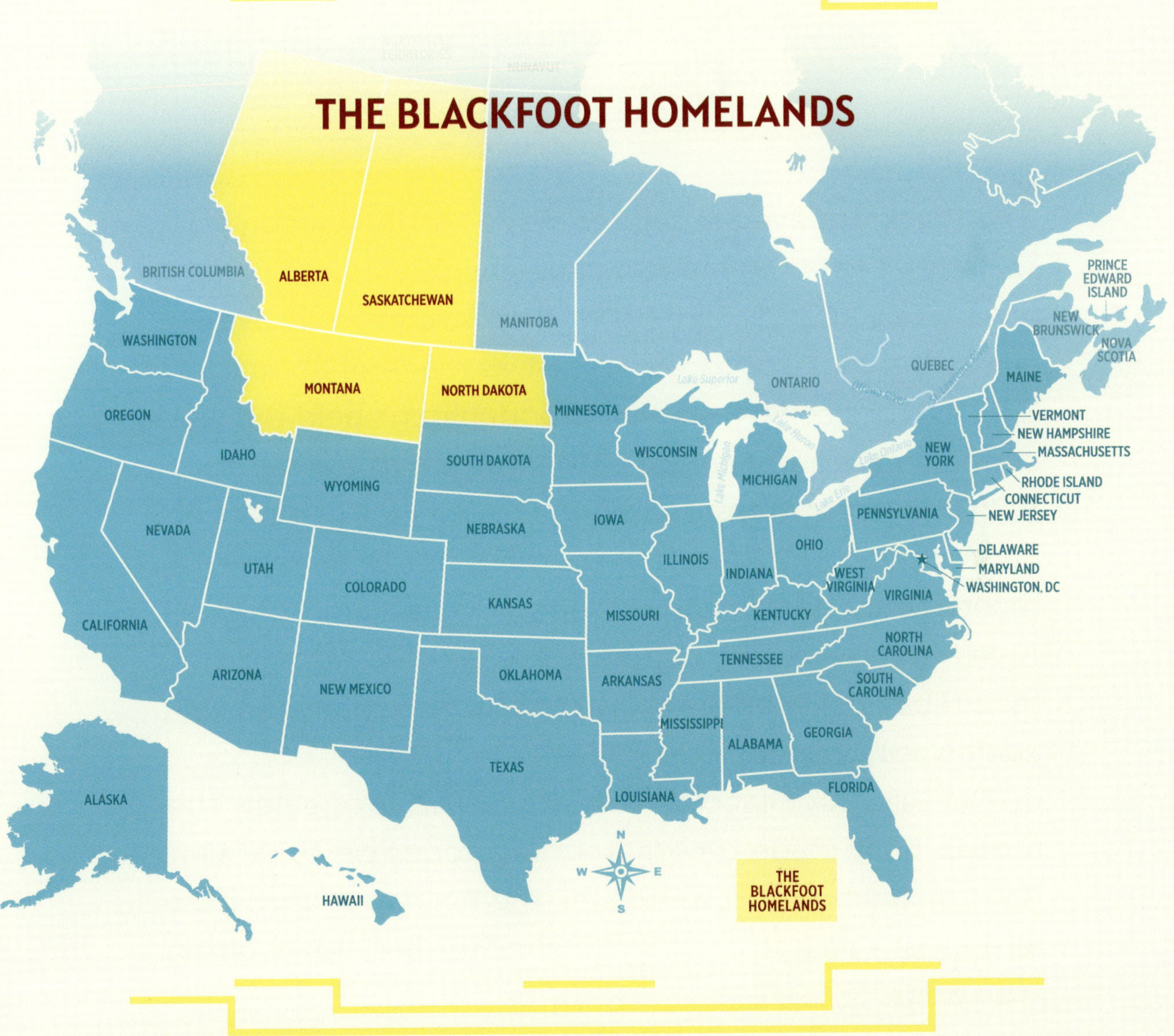
THE BLACKFOOT HOMELANDS
BRITISH COLUMBIA
ALBERTA
SASKATCHEWAN
MANITOBA
ONTARIO
QUEBEC
PRINCE EDWARD ISLAND
NEW BRUNSWICK
NOVA SCOTIA
WASHINGTON
OREGON
IDAHO
MONTANA
NORTH DAKOTA
MINNESOTA
WISCONSIN
MICHIGAN
NEW YORK
MAINE
VERMONT
NEW HAMPSHIRE
MASSACHUSETTS
RHODE ISLAND
CONNECTICUT
NEW JERSEY
DELAWARE
MARYLAND
WASHINGTON, DC
SOUTH DAKOTA
WYOMING
NEVADA
UTAH
COLORADO
NEBRASKA
IOWA
ILLINOIS
INDIANA
OHIO
PENNSYLVANIA
WEST VIRGINIA
VIRGINIA
KENTUCKY
CALIFORNIA
KANSAS
MISSOURI
TENNESSEE
NORTH CAROLINA
SOUTH CAROLINA
ARIZONA
NEW MEXICO
OKLAHOMA
ARKANSAS
MISSISSIPPI
ALABAMA
GEORGIA
TEXAS
LOUISIANA
FLORIDA
ALASKA
HAWAII
N
W
E
S
THE BLACKFOOT HOMELANDS

Homes

The Blackfoot lived in tepees made by the women's societies. First they made a cone-shaped frame with four poles. They added more poles, then stretched a cover across the frame. A tepee cover was made of about 15 buffalo hides sewn together. Wooden pegs held the cover closed and kept it in place at the bottom of the tepee.

In the winter, women lined the tepees with additional buffalo skins. The Blackfoot used fire pits to heat their tepees. They slept on beds made with buffalo fur robes.

In the summer, the people rolled up the bottoms of their tepee covers. This allowed breezes to blow through and cool the inside of the tepee.

The Blackfoot used **travois** (trav-WAHZ) to carry tepees. They made travois from two tepee poles. At first, dogs pulled these travois. Later, the Blackfoot used horses, which were able to carry more supplies and travel farther than dogs.

Not all tepees were painted. The Blackfoot believed that spirits gave images in dreams so that harmony and long life would come to those inside.

Food

The Blackfoot hunted and gathered their food. They hunted moose, elk, deer, rabbit, pronghorn, quail, and American bison, often called buffalo. Blackfoot hunters used bows, arrows, spears, and guns to kill their prey.

Buffalo were an important food source for the Blackfoot. Hunters with spears or arrows had to get close to a buffalo to kill one. To do this, hunters covered themselves with a buffalo **hide**. They approached the herd from downwind so the animals could not smell their scent.

The Blackfoot also used buffalo jumps. Hunters herded buffalo into a lane that ended with a steep cliff. When the buffalo stampeded down the lane, they ran off the cliff. Below, hunters and women waited to harvest the animals.

People either ate buffalo meat fresh or dried it for later use. They mixed the dried meat with wild berries, cherries, and buffalo fat to make pemmican (PEM-ih-ken). Pemmican could be stored and eaten later during travels.

Blackfoot women dried meat in the sun.

CHAPTER 5

Clothing

Blackfoot men wore buckskin shirts. The women sewed animal **hides** together to make the shirts. They decorated the shirts with **geometric** designs. They made the designs using porcupine **quills** or glass beads. Some shirts were decorated with weasel tails, which were a sign of bravery.

Men also wore **breechcloths** and thigh-high fringed leggings. The leggings protected their legs from brush and thorns while they were hunting.

Blackfoot women wore long dresses made from elk hides. They decorated the dresses with fringe, quills, beads, elk teeth, or cowrie shells. They wore wide belts decorated with geometric designs around their waists. Women carried their **awls** and knives on their belts.

In the winter, both men and women wore buffalo-hide robes to keep warm. They wore moccasins on their feet with soles painted black or darkened with ashes. Many people believe this is how the Blackfoot got their name.

Blackfoot men Medicine Wolf and Night Rider wearing deerskin dance clothing in 1936.

Crafts

The Blackfoot were excellent craftspeople. They used many natural materials in their crafts. They used rocks, plants, berries, clay, and ash to make paint. They also used the skins and other parts of animals, such as the buffalo.

Men carved buffalo bones and horns into cups and other tools. They painted **pictographs** on the inside of buffalo robes, as a way to record important Blackfoot events. Sometimes the men spread a robe out on the ground. They told the people the stories painted on the robe.

Women painted pictographs and **geometric** designs on the inside of tepee liners and covers. They also decorated clothing, bags, and belts. They used bone needles and **sinew** thread to sew beads and porcupine **quills** into beautiful geometric designs.

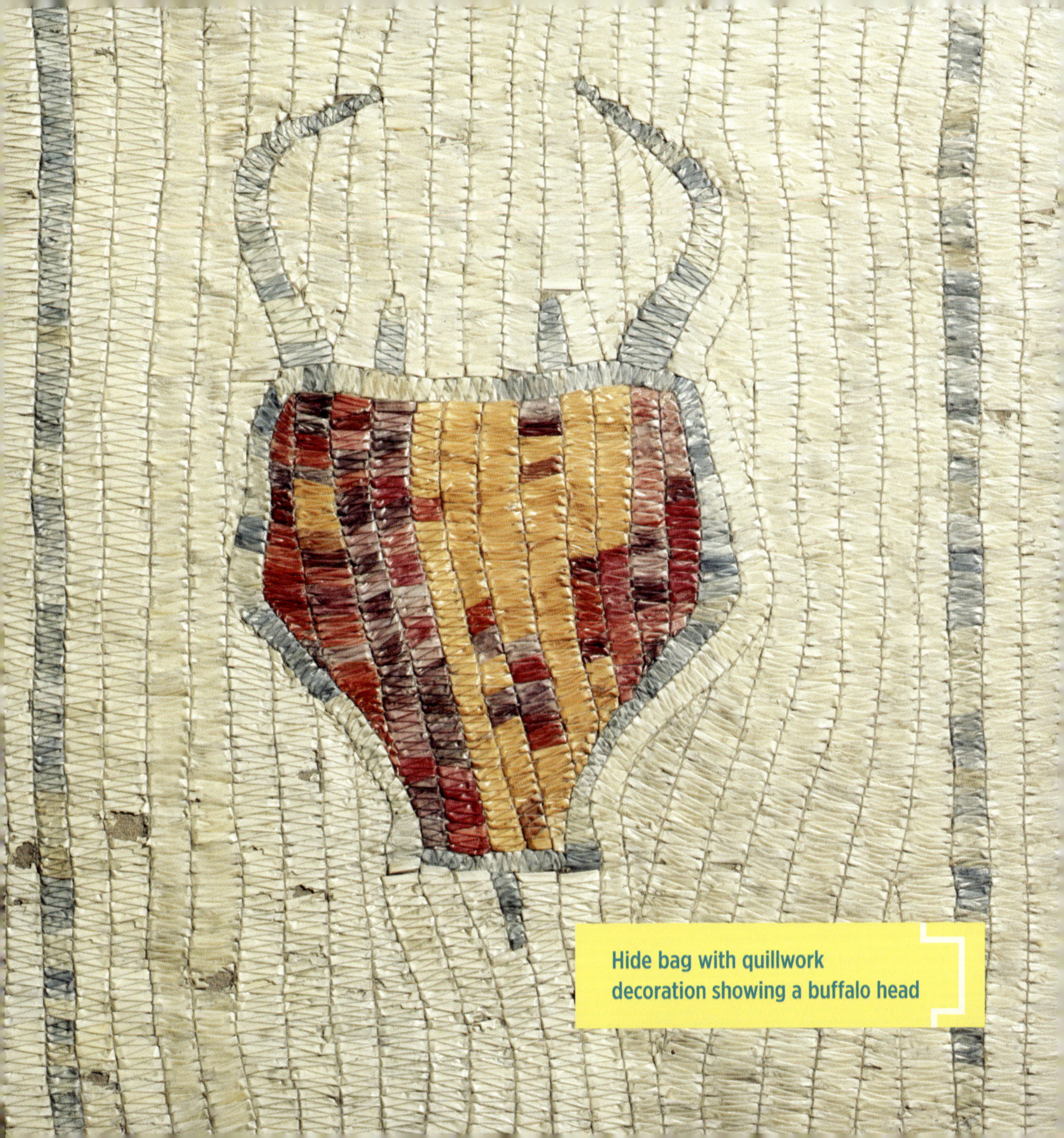

Hide bag with quillwork decoration showing a buffalo head

CHAPTER 7

Family

In Blackfoot families, men could marry more than one woman. Sometimes a man married his first wife's sisters. They all lived together in one tepee.

The first wife had authority over the other wives. She was called his "sits beside him wife," because she always sat to her husband's left side. The other wives sat to the left of the first wife.

The women took care of the children. They made clothing, cooked, and preserved food for the winter. When the hunters killed an animal, the women butchered it using stone knives. Sometimes, women joined the warriors to protect the people.

Men hunted buffalo and other animals. They made the weapons needed for hunting and protection. They also made spoons, cups, and other tools from buffalo horns, bones, and **hides**. Men sometimes made their own clothing.

The Blackfoot are loyal to their family and clan.

Children

Blackfoot children were an important part of the family. The whole family taught and protected them. The children learned much by helping their parents.

Boys learned how to make bows and arrows. They also played a game with a spoked hoop wrapped in **rawhide**. The boys rolled the hoop along the ground. They shot arrows through the hoop as it rolled. This game sharpened the boys' hunting skills.

Girls learned how to cook, prepare buffalo **hides**, and do **quill** and bead work. They also learned how to sew together hides to make small tepees. The tepees were large enough for the girls to play inside. This taught them how to build, care for, and move tepees.

Boys and girls went through a **rite of passage**. Elders performed a ceremony and gave instructions on adulthood. The boys and girls also sought a vision. Sometimes a spirit guide came to the child to help him or her throughout life.

Friends meet at the annual Blackfeet Nation North American Indian Days in Browning, Montana.

Traditions

The Blackfoot believe Napi (NAH-pee), or Old Man, created all living things. He gave humans and animals life. Napi also created land and food.

Napi placed each animal, bird, and plant in a special place that it was suited for. The bighorn sheep have special hooves made to climb steep cliffs. So Napi placed them in the mountains. The pronghorn could run very fast. So Napi placed them on the open prairie.

Napi also made human shapes from clay. He blew breath onto them to give them life. He showed the humans how to live on the land, what to eat, and where to find plants to heal sickness.

Napi created the buffalo. He showed the Blackfoot how to kill buffalo and use them to make food, clothing, tepees, and tools. When Napi had finished teaching the Blackfoot, he said he would always watch over the people.

Bighorn sheep live in the Rocky Mountains.

War

The Blackfoot were excellent warriors. During war, Blackfoot **bands** often joined together. The united warriors protected the people and land.

Warriors fought with many types of weapons. They used bows and arrows, stone knives, war clubs, and lances. The warriors made knife blades, arrowheads, and lance points from flint. They shaped them by hitting the flint with another rock.

Blackfoot men used shields for protection. They made the shields from stretched buffalo **rawhide**. They painted the shields and their horses with protective drawings.

A Blackfoot warrior could earn honors by counting coup on an enemy. This meant a warrior touched a sleeping enemy or took his weapon. The Blackfoot believed it took greater courage to count coup on an enemy than to kill him. A man who counted coup could earn his way into a respected military society.

Blackfoot warriors at Glacier National Park in Montana

Contact with Europeans

Spanish explorers brought horses to North America in the 1500s. By the 1700s, the Blackfoot received horses through trade with other tribes. Horses allowed the Blackfoot to travel farther, and made hunting buffalo safer.

Europeans traded goods such as guns, blankets, and alcohol for **hides** and decorated clothing. They also brought diseases. The Blackfoot did not have natural defenses against such diseases, so many people died.

In 1855, the Blackfoot and the US government signed a treaty. The treaty said the Blackfoot would receive food and trade goods if they allowed whites to travel across their lands. White settlers soon flooded into their lands.

White men hunted the buffalo to near extinction. By the winter of 1883-1884, the buffalo herds had disappeared. That winter, many Blackfoot starved to death.

Blackfeet Warriors Sculpture,
Blackfeet Indian Reservation, Montana

Crowfoot

Issapo'mahkikaaw (isah-poh-mah-ki-kah) was a respected Blackfoot leader. He was born around 1830 in Alberta, Canada. He was courageous in battle. Once, he was wounded while fighting the Crow. This is how he earned the name Crowfoot.

Crowfoot was not born into a family of chiefs. But he was a good speaker, and was well respected. He eventually became a chief of the Siksika.

As chief, Crowfoot worked for the health and safety of his people. He wanted the Blackfoot to stop drinking whiskey and other alcohol. He saw that his people were dying and being cheated.

Crowfoot believed it was best for the Blackfoot to make peace with other tribes, as well as white settlers and traders. In 1877, he signed Treaty Seven. In 1885, he kept his people from participating in the North-West Rebellion. He died in 1890, after a long illness.

Crowfoot in 1886

The Blackfoot Today

Today, many Blackfoot live on reservations. In the United States, the Blackfeet Reservation in Montana is home to the Pikuni, or South Piegan. In Alberta, Canada, the Siksika Nation, the Kainai Nation, and the Piikani Nation each have their own reserves.

The Blackfoot are working to protect their sacred lands. In 2023, they saved the Badger-Two Medicine area from being used for development and drilling. The Blackfoot wish to preserve the environment for the future.

The Blackfoot are working to preserve their **culture**, too. Apps have been created to help teach the language. Community colleges include Blackfoot culture and language in their programs. The Head-Smashed-In Buffalo Jump Interpretive Centre and Blackfoot Crossing Historical Park, both in Alberta, Canada, also provide information about the Blackfoot culture.

Actress Lily Gladstone wears a stand-up headdress. She is the first Indigenous person to win a Golden Globe for best actress.

Glossary

awl—a pointed tool for marking or making small holes in materials such as leather or wood.

band—a number of persons acting together; a subgroup of a tribe.

breechcloth—a piece of hide or cloth, usually worn by men, that is wrapped between the legs and tied with a belt around the waist.

confederacy—a group of people joined together for a common purpose.

culture—the customs, arts, and tools of a nation or people at a certain time.

geometric—made up of straight lines, circles, and other simple shapes.

hide—an animal skin that is often thick and heavy.

pictograph—a picture that represents a word or idea.

quill—a stiff, sharp hair or spine.

rawhide—untanned cattle hide.

reservation—a piece of land set aside by the government for Native Americans to live on.

rite of passage—an event or ceremony after which a child is considered an adult.

sinew—a band of tough fibers that joins a muscle to a bone.

travois—a frame of two wooden poles tied together over the back of an animal and allowed to drag on the ground. It was used to transport loads.

ONLINE RESOURCES

To learn more about the Blackfoot, please visit **abdobooklinks.com** or scan this QR code. These links are routinely monitored and updated to provide the most current information available.

Index

Badger-Two Medicine 28
bands 6, 22
bead work 12, 14, 18
Blackfoot Crossing Historical Park 28
buffalo 8, 10, 12, 14, 16, 18, 20, 22, 24, 28

ceremonies 6
chiefs 6, 26
children 16, 18
clothing 12, 14, 16, 20, 24
council of elders 6
counting coup 22
crafts 14, 22
culture 28

diseases 24

Europeans 24

family 16, 18
food 6, 10, 16, 18, 20, 24

games 18

Head-Smashed-In Buffalo Jump Interpretive Centre 28
homelands 4, 28
hunting 10, 12, 16, 18, 24

Issapo'mahkikaaw (Crowfoot) 26

Kainai 4, 28

language 4, 28

Napi 20
Niitsitapi 4
North West Rebellion 26

pictographs 14
Piikani 4, 28

quill work 12, 14, 18

religion 6
reservations 28
rites of passage 18

Siksika 4, 26, 28
societies 6, 8, 22
South Piegan 28

tepee 8, 14, 16, 18, 20
trade 24, 26
travel 8, 24
travois 8, 10
Treaty Seven 26

vision quest 18

war 16, 22, 26
weapons 10, 16, 18, 22, 24
white settlement 24, 26